To

M.n Chan:

May God continue to bless
you and keep you! I'm proud
of you and your Journey with
God.

Who is Your Moses?

In The Eyes of a Lad

By

Dr. Ronald S. Hobson

Love

Bishop

Scripture quotations are from the King James Version (KJV) or New International Version (NIV).

Printed in the United States of America

Book Cover Design by Jeffery Brower of Custom Made Graphics Design (CustomMadeGraphics@gmail.com)

Edited by Var Kelly of Var Ministries (VarMinistries@gmail.com)

ISBN: 978-0-578-19946-7

Dedication

This book is dedicated to my mother, Geraldine Scott. Without your womb, there would be no me! Because of your leadership in the home; and your acceptance and faith in Christ, you turned me over to The Spiritual Father & Moses of our family.

This book is also dedicated to my mentor and Pastor, Bishop Ralph Livingston Jefferson, DD., Senior Pastor & Founder of Jefferson Temple Church of God in Christ, North Bellport, New York. Thank you, Bishop! Your tenacity and resiliency of leadership will always cling dearly to my heart. You are a source of splendor and a tremendous gift to The Kingdom of God.

Lastly, this book is dedicated to my spiritual mother; Mother Ada M. Jefferson. You have worked tirelessly down through the years and you've never asked for any recognition. Also, you always supported the work of our pastor. You kept me on the right path. The conversations we had at church and at your house put me in check. Thank you, Mother Jefferson!

Table of Contents

Acknowledgements

First and foremost, to my Lord and Savior Jesus Christ - If it had not been for The Lord on my side, none of this would even be possible.

To my sons, Ron Jr., & Christopher - Life never came with instructions, but it often teaches us from our experiences. If time could change, many changes would be made. However, I thank God for the mother of my children, Theresa Hunter. Sons, your existence in my life is more precious than gold, and it's my prayer that you both continue to strive to be a tremendous asset to humanity.

To my mother, Mother Geraldine Scott, the family's source of splendor - Your wit, eagerness, patience, tolerance, genuine love, and commitment to our family is phenomenal. Your tenacious approach to life and education gave us the thriving force to continue to go forward in life. Mom, Thank You, for just being real, true, and yourself.

To the many great men and women of the cloth who also were instrumental in my overall training: Apostle Milton Malloy, Bishop Kenneth Davis, Bishop Sylvester Wright, Superintendent Ralphael Jefferson (My 1st Sunday School Teacher), Bishop Romelle Adams, Pastor Darlene Cobb, Pastor Nettie Ellison, Elder Cherra Culbreath, The late Elder Mildred Bieard and Deacon Leonard Habersham – you each compelled and provoked me in many ways and I am indeed grateful for you all.

To the many sons and daughters in the faith that I've had the privilege to pastor or mentor over the past 17 years of pastoral ministry: You and I can both acknowledge that there is no perfection in oneself, however, my desire was and still is to impart in you the values and Christian character that was afforded me by such a great cloud of witnesses on earth. The cloud of witnesses was my compass and guided me towards leadership. Every day was not a picnic in the park, but I tried to lead and guide you in a manner that was pleasing to The Lord.

To my dear friends, Elder Melvin James & Shelly Robinson - For many years you've both supported every ministry or work that was wrought through me by God. You have always demonstrated great love to me as if we were family.

To Courtney James Young - Thank you for the many times you drove me to preaching engagements. Your support was indeed a blessing.

To Overseer Henry Tindal Jr., and Presiding Bishop Henry A. & Mother Bishop Shirley Tindal – you three were placed in my life to refuel The Holy Ghost fire in me when ministry looked like it was taking a turn for the worse. To Overseer Henry Tindal, Jr. - from our first encounter at the water to you introducing me to your parents and United Fellowship of Christian Churches and Ministries (UFCCM); you all were placed into my life and embraced what The Lord placed in my life. You all are a thriving force to encourage me forward in all that I need to do for The Lord.

To my brothers and sisters; nephews and nieces, family and friends you are all dear to me and I love you all equally.

Special mention of:

- Pastor Seiji Thompson - thanks for being a true brother in the faith.
- Pastor Sherry L. Rice – thanks for your continuous support of my ministry and leadership since 2006. I pray that God's grace continues to abide in your life and ministry.
- Pastor Caleb T. Gordon – thanks for your true friendship of over 15 years. Your encouragement, guidance, and teaching pushed me to another level!
- Dr. Var Kelly - thank you for helping me in so many areas over the years. You were one of the supporters of me writing this book. At times I wanted to slap you because you kept pushing me, but I Thank God you did push me until this work was complete.

Foreword

Some leaders lead followers. Then, some leaders lead congregations. Yet, some leaders lead other leaders. This truth is what I have found through my friendship with Bishop R. Scott Hobson. He has been a constant support to not just me in my growth in leadership, but to countless other leaders I have met through him.

The wealth of knowledge given to him has been demonstrated through our many conversations and accomplished goals. Thus, when it was time for him to write his manuscript, I knew it would be an important mark in his life and a time of impartation to the world.

In this book, he shares a portion of knowledge given to him through much persecution, trials, and tribulations. While he has gone through much, he doesn't share this knowledge from a place of the victim. Instead, he shares it from a place of victory.

Dr. R. Scott Hobson shares counsel to those in need of advice; guidance for those who need to take action; instruction to those who need truth; and a warning to those who need to know the dangers and possible harms awaiting them. There is something in this book for everybody.

Hence, as you read allow The Holy Spirit to impart to you counsel, guidance, instruction and warning through the life of Dr. R. Scott Hobson.

Dr. Var Kelly, BA, BRE, MRE, DRE
Founder of Var Ministries,
New York, NY

Introduction

Leadership is not about the motivation to become someone special for the lights and pandemonium of many echoing your name. It is not about the ability to see how fortunate you have become to persuade others. Leadership is about the ability to show others the way, guide them and influence them in the right path of life.

For the past several years, I have watched many leaders rise and fall! The uniqueness of each of those leaders either thrust them to success or failure. As I perused The Scriptures to gather information concerning leadership, I found myself considering my life and my experiences. It was during this time of gathering information that my heart was steered towards the life of Moses.

In this work, my personal experiences before leadership and during leadership are discussed. Read about my childhood, my call to the ministry, and one of the most important decisions of my life.

Leaders of yesterday may not have the same situations to deal with today, but The Word of God is still the teacher of truth. Likewise, there are still lessons to learn from experiences from yesterday.

As you read these pages, note the lessons learned in each chapter through my life and that of Moses.

It's my prayer that this work will cause you and countless others to value the leadership God chooses you to carry out. I also pray that this book will become a teaching tool and reminder to all leaders during these final days.

—

Chapter One
The Background of a Leader

As we look at the introduction of Moses through the beginning of The Book of Exodus, there we discover opposition before he could even figure out who he was. In chapter two of Exodus, we discover that his life was introduced with significant trials and tribulations. However, The Lord had a plan for his life just like He has a plan for your life.

Moses was born in adverse conditions, and it's interesting to note that the adverse conditions were a setup. God sets us up for greatness even when we think there is nothing worth working for.

At birth, there was a decree by Pharaoh of Egypt to kill all newborn Hebrew males. The midwives, Shiphrah and Puah (Exodus 1:15) were charged to kill the Hebrew males. But the very fact that they feared The Lord, they did not follow through with the execution process of innocent Moses.

Imagine what these women were experiencing? They were choosing to disobey the highest man in authority. How many of us would have given in to the call of Pharaoh and followed through with his orders? These women showed their allegiance to The Lord despite what they could have faced. There is protection only The Lord can give when a detrimental decision must be made. Leaders must choose a wise and sound direction for those who will be following them. These women chose God, and this is key to leadership. Leaders, you must choose God first every time.

These two women chose to become types of United Nations (UN) officials for truth. Let me be the first to say; Mothers' you never know who you are raising, so nurture the gift that has been given to you either by birth or spiritual connection.

As we look a little further into the early adversity of Moses, we find that Jochebed, his mother, had tried to hide her son for three months. When she could no longer hide him, she placed him in a basket and then placed the basket on the Nile River (Exodus 2:2-3).

A mother is a nurturer and protector by instinct. Jochebed knew the child was a godly child and she had the faith that he would survive. Her instinct to nurture and protect kicked in to ensure safety for her child.

Remember, I said earlier that God would set us up for greatness in the midst of adversity? Well, while Moses was coasting in the midst of the river, the basket was picked up by the same family that put a hit out on the Hebrews. Pharaoh's daughter was bathing in the Nile River, and what catches her eye was a basket covered; distinct, fully wrapped and graciously presented. She reaches for the basket and uncovers to behold a male baby. There was no name, nor any instructions, but the child becomes a sparkle in her eye. Hence, she took the child out of the water, brought him to Pharaoh and asked could she keep him? He agreed and summoned a midwife (who was the child's birth mother) to breastfeed and care for the child.

Moses' mother was paid for raising her child. How many mothers would love that idea; getting paid to raise your child? Coming from the community that I was raised, the area of North Bellport, New York; the area had its share of adversities. There were tons of crime, political propaganda, civil debates, and an economic downfall that was out of control. Nevertheless, I know my mother; Geraldine Scott would have been thrilled to get paid for the nine children she birthed. Our economic infrastructure at the time of my youth was much similar to those of the Hebrews during the days of Moses. We were enslaved to the economic status quo; suffering in poverty; engulfed with the activity of working and not being able to reap a tremendous benefit for survival. I, being born premature, was destined for failure and there were no accomplishments predicted for my future. However, when you have been anointed to the work of The Lord, He will have situations and conditions arise so that He can get the glory.

In June of 1979, my family was in a horrific car crash that took the life of my only living grandmother. My grandfather, my mother, my sister Wanda, my brothers; Cornelius and Christopher and I were occupants of the car as well. Many of us suffered injuries from this accident because of a drunk driver. Through this experience, The Lord had a Man of God by the name of Ralph L. Jefferson, Pastor of Jefferson Temple, Church of God in Christ, Inc. (Bellport, New York) arrive at the scene and administer pastoral care. From this encounter, we became members of his church right after the funeral for my grandmother.

A disaster started our family's spiritual journey to Jesus. I became very fond of Pastor Jefferson, the affectionate name given to him. Never being part of a Pentecostal church before, I was excited to see him preach and jump over the rail when The Holy Ghost took over. Each Sunday was exciting and different. The music playing, the choir singing, and watching the saints praise God was awesome. I remember one particular Sunday our pastor was preaching and he grabbed me out to make an illustration, and I started crying because I felt overjoyed. From then on I wanted to be just like Pastor Jefferson. There was no father figure in my home, which was pretty common in our community. Yet, Pastor Jefferson became a spiritual father to me.

My mother raised all of her children to the best of her capabilities. We were never without food, clothing or shelter. My mother is a strong nurturer and a great example for all mothers to emulate. There were many occasions when she would walk to work in blizzards, rain, and heat -

18

fighting the elements just to provide for her children. While my mother was a mother and did her job, Pastor Jefferson was the authoritative male-figure I needed to guide me in the right direction. Similar to what Pharaoh's daughter did for Moses, at the age of nine; Pastor Jefferson was able to reach in the water of gloom and doom to pour into my life. I was picked up out of the water; out of the environment of despair.

God will never allow you to have an anorexic mentality when you are destined for a land flowing with milk and honey. If Moses was raised in the reality of the conditions of his day, he might have been consumed with the many affiliating tragedies of the people. Before The Lord places us in any society, He prepares us mentally, physically, emotionally and spiritually. Moses was prepared in Pharaoh's house for greatness. Similarly, I was prepared and grew in God at the hands of Pastor Jefferson.

The name Moses was given to the child. His name means drawn out of the water. When we give names to our children, give names that are meaningful and powerful. As I researched my name, it means - strong, leader, bright, powerful and kingly. WOW!

Moses' life in Pharaoh's care changed his conditions for the better. Like Moses, God will place us where we can learn and mature in the areas that He will drive us to through His Spirit.

The lifestyle of Moses imparted to him royalty, connected to a family that wanted for nothing! What an ideal situation; living above your means at the expense of others. Yes! This is ideal and very inviting to many. However, there is a price that is required when being prepared by God for leadership.

I didn't have a father in my life, but my situation became ideal when Pastor Jefferson came into my life. I was able to receive instructions from a spiritual father. I could remember one occasion when I was with Pastor Jefferson, and he gave me certain instructions. Processing the instructions was hard for me. Likewise, sometimes executing them were even harder. However, my leader would take the time to instruct and reiterate the information to me. That was a huge help. It helped me to understand better what was required. Of course, there had to be a form of repetition with me to process. I am sure my pastor could have chosen other's to pour into and to nurture; however, I am grateful for the grace and mercy of our Lord, my leader stuck with me, and now I am pushing others to become all for The Lord.

Moses had to face many challenges in his life one of which included a speech impediment – stuttering. Taking a bird's eye view of my preparation to leadership there were many obstacles - mentally, physically, emotionally, and most of all spiritually – all of which I had to face and conquer. Most of my challenges dealt primarily in the physical and mental state. Two of these challenges included the effects of premature birth and being a slow learner. Nevertheless, I had to overcome. As I grew, I learned to overcome these obstacles. Some things took longer for me to overcome. Yet, I travailed and conquered many things early in life.

Reviewing the background of my life and that of Moses helped me to realize that God always had a plan for my life. I challenge you to view the background of your life. Don't just see the bad and terrible times. Reflect on the good as well. Reflect on the grace of God that manifested in your life. Reflect on the day when the gun fire was heard, but the bullet didn't hit you. When the death angel was at the door, but God said no; when the judge meant to say guilty, but God made them say innocent. Reflect and remember for in understanding your background; it will help you understand where you're going.

Chapter Two
The Call to Leadership

If you were to ask the average leader, "Do you think you were prepared to lead people?" It's likely many would probably say, "No!" I've come to realize that preparation for leadership begins when a person becomes a responsible follower. A normal follower would watch their leader, but not seek a personal relationship with their leader. A responsible leader will serve God and their leader. They would know how to be seen and not heard and even ask questions when appropriate. Being a responsible follower is key in the development of leadership. As I reflect on my 16 years of time spent with Pastor Jefferson, following and studying him, I can truly say I was a responsible follower. One thing I never saw him do in any situation was sweat over things. To this day, when situations come my way that aren't ideal, I don't sweat it.

In the call of leadership for Moses, we find that he had personal contact with God himself at the burning bush (Exodus 3). At this pivotal point, it could have been easy for Moses just to tell God no. An answer of no is easy to say when humanity calls you, but when you are called out specifically by The Lord, the response of no is not an option. Despite Moses' attempt to back up and out of the call, he gave God a yes. It's always easy for leaders who are called to back up instead of stepping forward. Leaders can often second guess their abilities because of their past, failures, or low self-esteem. Yet, the more the leader tells God yes, the more change comes and more relevant their ministry calling.

The question that pops in my mind is, "Can a leader ever really be prepared to lead?" I've learned that it's easy only if the leader allows them self to be broken. At the age of 14, I was placed in the position as Junior Deacon at our home church. This was my launch into leadership. This was the first time anyone had even thought of putting me in any leadership role. Although many would like to believe it was minor, it was major to me because someone believed in me. I was given responsibilities and tasks to complete in a timely manner. I served as an usher, choir member and pastor's helper all at the same time. I believe my pastor was teaching me to be a multi-tasker. While staying close to him, I was able to learn not only how to serve, but to be committed to studying The Word of God. For many years, I knew in advance where I would be; Tuesday, Friday and all day Sunday. Where was I? I was in church. My routine did not change much for many years. I had to mow the grass at the church, paint, clean, witness, travel and all as a Junior Deacon. Then, on top of that – I still had school work and my responsibilities at home. You see for me, leadership is not a picnic in the park. It is work.

In my experiences with my mentor, I found myself telling God yes to His call upon my life. Although I was just a Junior Deacon, I was being shaped and molded. This was true for Moses. While The Scriptures doesn't say much of his youth, he grew up and received training from those in Pharaoh's palace, but it took his wilderness experience when he left Egypt for God to shape and prepare him for the call to leadership.

Reflecting on the glorious day when I was called to the ministry; I remember we were in revival at our church. It was at the end of October 1988. It was a Saturday evening! My body was tired from the activities of the day. I can recall the dream I had. In the dream, I remember swallowing pages of a book. I remember the bittersweet taste even during the dream. At the moment, I didn't have a full understanding of the dream, so I figured there was no bother for me in sharing the dream with anyone. So, I kept it supposedly to myself. I can recall my pastor calling a prayer line that Sunday morning! As my pastor was praying, he stepped back, looked at me! And said, "You had a dream last night." The next words that uttered out of his mouth were, "Son, The Lord has called you to preach." Apparently, I was flawed because I still didn't understand what had just taken place. However, this day shaped my history and forged me to go forward with The Lord.

As that day marked the start of my process into ministry, there were many times when I felt like I couldn't handle the critical responsibilities and situations required for leadership. As I was put to the test by God, I was able to handle it. God did the same with Moses. When Moses said, "...they will not believe me, nor hearken unto my voice..." The Lord tested Moses to see if he was able to believe fully. God turned a rod into a snake, turned Moses' hand from well to leprosy, and turned water to blood (Exodus 4:1-9). Although Moses did not want to answer the call, his obedience in even obeying God's instructions allowed him to be tested.

During times when I knew I was being put to the test, I had to remain obedient to God, integral and honest. I know there were times when I gave my mentor a hard time in many areas; however what I am most appreciative about is that he never threw me to the curb. Even when I messed up, he would correct, and rebuke me in love. During those times, I just thought he was mean, but now that I am a leader, Pastor Jefferson was only preparing me for the challenging days ahead!

As God was preparing Moses to lead the people, I was prepared for leadership. To be effective in leadership, one must pay attention to detail. One of my greatest fears was not carrying out what my pastor asked me to do. It seemed so hard for me to pay attention to detail to the letter, which got me yelled at on many occasions. If I could impart anything to young and upcoming leaders today, it would be this: Listen to the instructions of your leader very closely.

Never get to a place where anyone cannot teach you anything. The youth of today tend to believe the older generation does not know anything about being young. I always have to tell them, "Hello?! The older generation is older. However, they were young before. They have already experienced what you're experiencing." There is an opportunity to learn from the leadership you sit under.

Chapter Three
The Work of Leadership

My work as a Junior Deacon was intense and long-lasting. It increased and intensified. On many occasions, I would hear my pastor say, "Son... The Bronx cannot whip brains." For many years, I sat and tried to figure out what he was trying to say. It wasn't until I got a little older that I understood what he was trying to convey to me. People from New York know that people from The Bronx are go-getters. They work hard for whatever they desire. They demonstrate great strength. However, sometimes knowledge is missing in their pursuit. I learned in order to be successful, not only must a leader be a go-getter – strong – they must gain knowledge. I believe that every leader desires to succeed. It will take knowledge and strength for success to occur.

Pastor Jefferson poured knowledge into me, and I am forever grateful. The knowledge given helped the strength I had to move forward into success with leadership.

Fears of Leadership
I believe success was one of Moses' greatest fears. He allowed the fear of success to make him believe he was unable to do his job effectively. At the burning bush, Moses said to The Lord, "...Who am I, that I should go unto

Pharaoh, and that I should bring forth the children of Israel out of Egypt?" (Exodus 3:11). Moses was thinking in his flesh; in his own abilities to deliver the people out of Pharaoh's control. Moses' attempt to think in his own power reminds me of a saying a pastor once told me. He said, "If you are not nervous before you preach, don't preach because you are in your flesh." The person in the quote is obviously over confident and therefore in their flesh. On the other side of the spectrum, we have Moses afraid of success because he never experienced it. Leaders of today cannot be confident in their abilities nor be so fearful of what God wants to do through them. You have to see your abilities empowered by The Hand of God at all times.

God assured Moses that he could do the job and that He would be there for him. God did this by manifesting His presence upon Moses. The presence of God is always comforting to any leader preparing to go to the next level. No good leader should make any move unless they have received the green light from the boss – God, Himself. Confirmation or Affirmation solidifies the call of a leader. The Word tells us in the mouth of two or three witnesses let every word be established (Matthew 18:16). Do not be eager to move unless God's presence is with you.

Another fear Moses demonstrated is common to many leaders of today. He was fearful of what the people of God would think and say about him. As previously stated,

Moses said, "...Who am I...that I should bring forth the children of Israel out of Egypt?" (Exodus 3:11). This is a typical leadership flaw that leaders deal with. They worry about what others think about them or how they value them. While God makes the selection of the leader, the picking and choosing of leadership has become a huge political mess in the church. Instead of God choosing the leader, it's now based upon who is the most popular. With that said let us take a moment and reflect on the choosing of David to be king of Israel.

God was displeased with the leadership of King Saul, and He was ready to replace him. In 1 Samuel 16:1, The Lord asked Samuel, "How long will you mourn for Saul, since I have rejected him as king over Israel?" When you as a leader are rejected by the most loving and caring God, you are in serious trouble. In our day, if you observe leaders who were gifted and anointed to lead and then, you begin to see them wavering in their faith; standby because a fall is imminent. These words may be a little harsh, but they speak the truth.

The Prophet Samuel was chosen to go to Jesse's house to anoint a new king. It was God who decided who would be king. It wasn't the people, what they thought of the king, or if they were *over* his leadership rule – it was The Lord who had ordained a shift to occur and not the people. Thus, you as a leader cannot be fearful of what people will say. You must respond to the call to lead from God.

31

I also must note another quote from a great mentor and father of The Gospel, Apostle Milton Malloy, II (Senior Pastor of Straight Up Christian Outreach Ministries). During my time of fellowship with him at his church in Philadelphia, Pennsylvania, he shared these words with me, "Son, if it makes sense, it's not God." What God was asking Samuel to do made no sense. Israel still had a king. Why should Samuel anoint one while there was a king still in office? As stated in Deuteronomy 29:29, "The secret things belong to God..." You can become fearful because of what God says, yet if it was God who said it, then you must follow through with it. Our fears like that of Moses don't matter to God. We must fear God when He speaks to us even when it doesn't make sense. The Prophet Samuel followed God's instructions and filled his horn with anointing oil and went to Jesse's home to anoint a new king.

Sacrifice is Required

As previously stated, what God told Samuel to do didn't make sense. Samuel had to sacrifice what made sense for what God said.

On countless occasions, many leaders said to me, "Don't let your left hand know what your right hand is doing." Samuel took the focus off of what made sense – his left hand and focused on what God said – his right hand. Samuel was willing to jeopardize his life to do what The

Lord asked him to do. He was willing to give up what made sense to him to do what God wanted him to do.

There will come the point in a leader's life - if they are true to the call – when they will sacrifice all for God. The ideal leader will sacrifice something in their own lives to see the will of God done, and others flourish. Scarifies will be required.

God Makes the Choice

The process of being chosen by God is not like that of humanity. If Jesse could have had his way, one of his sons other than David would have been his choice for a king. Like any other father/mother would do, Jesse paraded all his sons except David before the prophet. God had a process and had chosen who He knew was the one. Thus, as directed by The Lord, Samuel turned down all that Jesse presented. The word declares humanity looks on the outward appearance while God looks at the heart (I Samuel 16:7). After much wasted time, Samuel had asked Jesse, "Are here all thy children?" Jesse replied, "There remaineth yet the youngest, and, behold, he keepeth the sheep" (1 Samuel 16:11).

Unfortunately, David was not Jesse's first choice. Always remember, who you think is capable of leading may not be the one God chooses. We as people make the mistake of choosing leaders based on: looks, friendships, obligations, and age. While the thought behind the selection process

33

makes some sense, it's not how God operates. When will we as humans get a grasp or full concept of who God is? He is Omni – He is Everything. Before we even think about it, it was spoken by Him. With that said, Jesse was ordered by the prophet to send for the one he did not want to present. When David appeared, The Lord spoke to Samuel and said: "Arise, anoint him: for this is he." (I Samuel 16:12). Our spiritual characteristics should always outweigh our natural intentions. Quite naturally, we all look for success! It's natural. But when we try to downgrade those whom God has already sanctioned, we only put ourselves at a disadvantage with God.

Broken but Consistent
There were four major characteristics Moses demonstrated. He was:

- Willing to be with God,
- Willing to be humble and honest with God,
- Hungry and thirsty for more of God,
- And willing to be broken by God.

To be broken seems to be a major component of successful leadership. As I reflect back on my adolescent days, I remember how Pastor Jefferson trained me. Since he has received many commendations including a Purple Heart and is a Korean War Veteran, I now understand how he was developing me. His methodology was rough and stern at times; however, his bark was bigger than his bite.

Mentally, I not only had to be broken from my thinking, but I also had to be de-programmed from the streets.

When I share with people my upbringing in North Bellport, New York, they understand that there was a certain level of street smarts you had to have in dealing with the elements of the community. The community was almost like a pot of crabs in boiling water. The only way out was to grab and climb your way to the top while pulling or pushing someone else down.

One of my greatest examples was my very own brother, Kevin. He didn't claw his way to the top, but he was consistent in his approach to life. There were nine of us siblings: Wendy, Cheryl, William, Bryan, Kevin, Wanda, myself, Cornelius, and Christopher. Kevin always had a plan to get out of North Bellport. He envisioned himself not staying in our community when he graduated from High School. I remember watching him playing football, running track and playing other sports to occupy his mind. Also, he would cut hair, do odd jobs; work with the community leaders and the like to bring change for him and the family. I remember on many occasions he tried to help me with my homework. At the same time, he always saw himself doing better and more. When the time of decision came, he decided to further his education in college. I believe he was the first in our family to go to college. His consistency and drive to want to come out from where he was and be separated encouraged me to be consistent despite the brokenness that had taken place in my life. If you want change you have to do something different; something that you have never done before.

I looked up to all of my brothers because each of them had a unique position in my life. Nevertheless, Kevin was determined not to become another statistic of a black man murdered or in prison. The crime that protruded the streets of our community had a dismal effect on many hearts. Like an eagle is thrust into the air by its mother, so was the idea of Kevin flying away to attend Fredonia State College. Leaders have to be determined to be consistent even when the odds of survival are almost obsolete.

The ability to steer your life in the direction of success is based on how consistent you are. As a leader in training or even after becoming a leader, you must be consistent in doing the right things in the process. You can't allow your broken past – whether rich or poor – determine how consistent you are with reaching your future.

Price to Pay
If you ever take the time to listen to the many leaders that have contributed in some form or fashion to shape this world, many would probably share that they suffered until they could master what they were trying to achieve. Suffering is the source to prepare one for a bright outlook on life. Many aspiring leaders of this day love to look at the glitz and glamour of leadership; the nice cars, multi-million

dollar homes, money and jewelry and the like. However, there is some suffering.

You will have your portion of pain and suffering. There will be the loss of a family member or members, maybe some health issues, definitely some sleepless nights and some long hours of studying. There will also be manipulation of society. Manipulation may be a harsh word when dealing with leadership; however, it is part of the process. Success is based on the mind manipulation. Either you will say to yourself I am better than the environment I was brought up in, or just sit there and wish all that you could do after the fact.

True dreams are not just going to happen with the inner ability to want to succeed. We must take those dreams and work them out; make them into a vision. The vision sets forth the momentum of the mission. Then the mission helps to revolutionize our mindset and push us to success. Kevin was able to take his current situation of negativity and economic woes, and turn it into survival and commitment. This drive resulted in him graduating from college, retiring from the military and has made a comfortable life for him and his family.

The work of leadership is a process. You must deal with your fears and let them go. You have to be willing to fear The Lord and work what He has called you to do. In the process, you will have to make sacrifices. Being chosen isn't easy. There will be many moments when you are broken but you must be consistent.

I am a Facebook junky and love to read the ideas of those men and women who are in leadership roles. While sitting in my office on a very cold December morning, I was listening to a wonderful woman of God. As she gave wonderful illustrations about individuals called to leadership, I was inspired and went to Facebook to share this inspiration. I wrote this status:

"I was listening to a preacher on television this morning. They pointed something out of great significance. Those who were chosen to carry out an assignment had to wait many years to grow into the character of their position. In other words, the waiting time is the pruning time for success!"

It was many years before David became King of Israel. Yet, during that process The Lord was pruning him and preparing him for the work he was chosen to do. This is true for Moses. His years with Pharaoh and years before seeing the burning bush were a part of the process and preparation time.

If you stay committed to God's process, the work of leadership will be the work of The Lord manifested in your life.

Chapter Four
Personal Testimony of a Leader

In 1995 a few days after the death of my baby brother; Christopher, I was thrust into having to accept the death of my baby brother. His death brought a new meaning of accepting what God allows. Although, I was in church, singing in the choir, ushering on the usher board, and assisting the pastor in any area possible, my brother's death became one of the ongoing personal issues I had to deal with.

For many in our community, young men in the community had no real help, and they were being killed left and right. Death had become a type of monthly ritual. There were no words of comfort for the embattled community faced with so much despair.

Our family was very well respected in our community. We were not materially wealthy, but very well-mannered and appreciative of what people had done for us. Our mother always showed all of her children love and nurtured us to be productive citizens of society. No, I am not saying we were the perfect family. Like any other family around, there were weaknesses in the very fiber of this tight fit family. Our weaknesses were made perfect in knowing who Christ was in our lives.

Reflecting on the hours leading to that very depressing call, earlier that morning my sister - Wanda, Christopher a.k.a. Chrissy and I were watching Soul Train. We were clowning on the dancers. We were simply laughing and joking as we normally would do. Outside, the sky was full of the bright summer sun with the fragrance of fresh cut grass permeating the atmosphere. The morning was the usual. Chrissy went to get a glass bowl and the box of cornflakes. Then, he would mash'em down! He would do what he knew best – eat. It was a typical day. Afterwards, we went our several ways for the day.

Although this all took place while I was in a backslidden condition, I remember the night too well. I was with a few friends. We were preparing to go hang out. The establishment that we were trying to get into would not let us in because someone wore boots. Nevertheless, we decided to just chill-out around the venue. I remember vividly constantly telling my friends, "I have to go home!" I sensed that something was wrong. I couldn't shake that feeling most of the night. Maybe they didn't take me home because I was under the powers of Hennessey or Old English. Despite my condition, I knew something was not right. The remainder of the night, I just kept on telling my friends, "I need to go home." Before they took me home, we went to the Patchogue Ave Park, parked on the side of the street and were listening to music. It was about 1:30 am in the morning. Then, finally, they took me home. My mother had not too long come in from visiting family earlier in the day. I crept into the house and eased on the couch because I knew I would receive some words from my mother for coming in that late.

After finding that comfortable spot on the couch, I laid down in which I thought would be a restful sleep. Around 2:30 am in the morning the phone rang in the kitchen, I rushed to the phone because I did not want it to wake up my mother. As I answered the phone, the individual stated, "Your brother has just been shot, and they are rushing him to the hospital." They stated, "We are coming over to get you and take you to the hospital."

At the moment, I was scared and somewhat speechless. I thought to myself, "How do I tell my mother that her baby son who has just graduated from High School two weeks ago that he's been shot?" I went to her room, and I remember her face and emotions as I shared with her what had happened. She began to shake. I told her to call my sister, Wendy and meet me at the hospital. I have always had to console other families and many friends, but I never thought that our day would come.

My brothers' friends came to the house and took me to the hospital. At the hospital there was a lot of commotion, people crying, attitudes flaring, anger rising and I was there all alone. I was alone for a short period, but it felt like an eternity. I thought to myself, "Here I am at the hospital where most of us were born in, and many of us have transitioned from." While I was experiencing bittersweet memories, I still was there alone. I recall the doctors asking me who I was as it related to my connection to Chrissy. As I told the doctor that I was one of the older brothers and that my mother and family were on the way, he told me something that haunts my mind to this day. It occasionally repeats in my mind and even brings me to tears as I type it. The doctor told me, "His chance for survival is 60/40." I said to him, "This is good right?!?" And the doctor told me, "He's losing too much blood."

By this time I was emotionally distraught because this young man in the surgery room was my baby brother whom we all loved. Chrissy was an accomplished track and field runner; breaking many records and aspired to run in the Olympics one day. And now his life was hanging in the balance of time.

After a while, my mother and family members rushed into the emergency room area. From that point, I was relieved to see our family's strength through my mother. Although her heart was torn, she managed to keep all of us happy and began to have us reflect on the many happy times and laughs we had. I remember mommy asking someone to call our pastor. Within a few minutes, he and Mother Jefferson came through the doors. What a relief to see them. It was added comfort to a delicate situation. There was a source of comfort when I saw these two powerful people of God come in the room – and to this day – any room. The clock was drawing later and later in the morning. My mother, however, kept going back and forth to get reports and updates on the condition of my brother. All in the lobby there was praying and constant speaking of the great things Chris had done. He was a giver, loved the disadvantaged and the less fortunate. If Chrissy knew you did not have something, it was not hard for him to give what he had. This was the way our mother trained us.

At the request of our family, we asked our pastor to go and pray for Chrissy. It was a blessed assurance to hear from our pastor that he lead our brother to salvation and there was a response from Chrissy acknowledging our Lord and Savior. Moreover, nothing could prepare all of us for what we would hear next.

All of us are familiar with the usual TV scene when the doctor calls the whole family into the *famous* room of gloom and doom. We were all asked to come in the room, they asked was there anything they could get us, and then the bombshell came. "We've done all we could do. He did not make it!" explained the doctor. This was all I heard. Immediately I got up, hit the wall and ran out the room! I cannot grasp what happened the last few moments after that. The baby boy was gone!

From this experience of hurt, our family was thrust into another area. We had to lead by example despite not knowing what the cause of why we had to experience such pain. My mother exemplified the most notable character. She somehow kept the family together. Many of us wanted to go after who may have been involved, but we had no true knowledge. This gallant Woman of God had us to pray and ask The Lord to reveal the perpetrators involved. Mom embraced us all and said, "Let's get through this together." I had never seen such gracefulness than what I witnessed through my mother. The community was in an uproar. People coming back and forth to the house, telegrams, flowers, food, and money - all just poured in. At the same time, the matriarch of our family positioned all of her children to love, pray and show others what to do in the midst of adversity.

As the final two days approached before the funeral, we had to prepare to say our final good-bye. At the wake, people were lined up all around the funeral home and at the home-going celebration. People were wall to wall, and hundreds of people were outside of our home church - Jefferson Temple Church of God in Christ. There were mourners from far and near, black and white, from across the street to across the tracks. People flocked to pay homage and respect. There were many kind words echoed throughout the sanctuary. However, the most difficult part for me was to sing my brother's favorite song originally sung by Rev. Timothy Wright titled, "Trouble Don't Last Always." Chrissy loved for me to sing that song, and I never sang it again since the day of his funeral.

From this tragic experience, it increased my desire to serve as a leader again. I was wrapped in pain, and my heart was broken. I did not want to be a part of the church world anymore. So, I decided to go into the United States Army. I enlisted at the age of 26, to try and deal with my brother's death, a new marriage and the idea of trying to be a father. It was too overwhelming for me. By going to the military, I thought it would be ideal and that it would give me a tremendous start. Not so!

When we make decisions, they should be based upon assets. How can you benefit from making such moves, and how does it affect those who are close to you? I had every reason to leave as I thought. This was further from the truth. Environmental changes will come and place you at a point of valuable decision making and not the destruction of your very character. When we do not consult God, we insult Him.

I reflect on The Scriptures of Proverbs 3:5-6. It says, "Trust in The Lord with all thine heart and lean not unto thine own understanding. In all thy ways acknowledge Him, and He shall direct thy paths." At this most pivotal decision-making point in my life, I did not trust The Lord. To this day, I try to consider and search why I entered the military at such an age, but at the time I was not concerned about others - just me! I have learned to understand that hurt people, hurt other people. That is a course that I would recommend to any leader not to follow suit with. Once you start on that journey, the trick of the devil will constantly play with your mind. The focus of your life becomes bleak, dark and gloomy. It's almost like having a cataract disease without knowing that you were seeing clear the whole time.

Leadership is not just a visual thing. It's a heart motivating factor. Although, many situations may push you to that specific area, wait to get clear, definitive directions from the one that has called you into such an awesome level of maturity. Many people this day are looking for quick fixes for permanent problems. Never allow your emotions and ill feelings to prompt you to lead if you have not effectively taken on the responsibility to follow.

My whirlwind account - from the death of my baby brother to me enlisting into the army - is similar to Moses' attempt to flee from what he had done. In Exodus 2:13-15, Moses fled from the face of Pharaoh because he killed an Egyptian. He fled for his life. Moses had no idea that God had a bigger and much larger plan for his life. Like Moses, I knew only a part of God's plans for me in leadership. With persistence and commitment to God, little by little, things were revealed to me.

It was the work of The Holy Spirit that wrought out my bad decision and created in me a clean, new heart.

Chapter Five
Leadership for TODAY

Viewing the life of Moses through a spiritual magnifying glass, it caused me to believe that although he did not understand the voice, he understood the call of God. From the burning bush and forward, he had to learn to understand the voice of God while responding to the call of God.

Leaders of today can only be effective in ministry by seeing the focal and vocal points of what they're doing. They have to deal with and learn about God along the way or disaster is sure. For Moses, he struck the rock when God said speak to the rock (Numbers 20:7-12). This experience is the type of buckle many leaders face while answering the call of God. They think they know where they're going, but then they hit a buckle. It takes a while before a buckle is produced in a road, and for a long time Moses had never dealt with the constant bickering he heard from the people of Israel. Thus, as this anger built up, it caused a buckle to produce along the road. This buckle of life impacted his life so much until he could not enter into the very Promised Land he was sent to lead the people into. Leaders of today must be willing to deal with issues that arise when they reveal them self. If they don't, a buckle can develop on the road. Don't let anything hinder your movement into what God promised you.

Tell the Truth

At the burning bush, Moses mentioned that he felt that he was not capable of handling the great assignment set before him. I can appreciate his willingness to admit his shortcomings. Many leaders in this day act as if they are not successful until they have hundreds or even thousands to lead. I find this hard to absorb in my spiritual mindset.

As I look at the life of Jesus, His ministry was unique. His style should be adopted by every believer. Nowhere in The Scriptures will we find that Jesus evangelized in the temple or synagogues. The focus was to reach the un-churched, the downtrodden, and broken-hearted. Our ultimate goal should be to reach those who have not yet heard The Gospel and disciple them to do the same – reach others with The Gospel. As Pharaoh was introduced to the true God through the acts and voice of Moses, people today will be introduced to the true God by how you act and by your voice.

If you question your tactics on reaching the lost, try revisiting The Scriptures. Jesus was able to lead them to God through Him. He lead by example and has given us all a blue-print or pattern as to how we should lead people to God through Him.

Why is it that many leaders are eager to lead, but never eager to spend quality time preparing for the days ahead? I am so afraid of popcorn preachers in this day and time. So many want to become a bishop, prophet, pastor, apostle, evangelist or teacher, but they never worked in The Kingdom. So many want to be a Kingdom Builder but never worked The Kingdom Principles. As we study the life of our Savior, He called His disciples out of their situations to learn of Kingdom Principles and turn to a godly mindset.

Tell yourself the truth. If you need help, get help. Don't be so fast until you miss the mark and fall into sin. Be willing to follow Jesus and preach, teach and live The Truth. What's The Truth? The Truth is that Jesus Christ saves. There is hope. Let your life be a living sacrifice to The Lord and an example for the people among you.

Work While It is Day

As we journey through this life as living epistles, let's have enough work behind us to validate our claim as servants. It is very alarming on how many leaders are under a certain age. Our leaders of today are more enthused about a name and not character. They desire to have material gain and no integrity. It is my opinion and heartfelt press to believe that God is calling for people that will follow Him to the letter. We must not be hearers only but also doers of The Word (James 1:22). The compelling factor to this leadership movement is the willingness to serve.

Remember, as Jesus taught his followers, He took the time to nurture and impart. I am convinced that the more time we spend sitting at the feet of a good leader; the impartation will be more rewarding. All but one of the disciples fully understood the character and personality of Jesus – His Spirit and nature. You will always notice which mentee has sat at the feet of their mentor. There will be some identifying marks and vocal language that will automatically note who they are following. It should not be surprising that there is a notable spiritual DNA.

I am proud to say that I act somewhat like my spiritual father in The Gospel! When you have followed well, their words may be a constant reminder of staying on the right track and doing the right thing! I often can hear the echo of my pastor constantly telling me, "Don't do that." Apostolic fathering is not just a whim, but an apostolic privilege given by our Lord Jesus Christ! Too many leaders take this as just an act and not a responsibility. Many leaders want people to submit to their authority, but never take the time to be submissive to a leader.

The nucleus disciples – The 12 disciples - had a great advantage. They daily received from Jesus direct impartation. This is a vital tool and spiritual mandate. Too many bastards are walking around with falsified validations and encrypted documentation without authentic representation. There are so many who claim to be authentic and real, and when proper investigations are done, you find no one has ever heard of their character. Most of them are just classified as *characters*.

Be true to yourself. Be comfortable with who you are in God. Work the work God has called you to. If you note, God chose many individuals in The Bible who were about their business and work. Peter and John were fishermen. Paul was a tent maker. David was a shepherd. Matthew was a tax collector. These men along with countless other men and women were doing their work or going about their work when they were called. This is important for you as well. I have never seen so many people who decide that they must be the man or the woman before they have even reached their 40th birthday. It can take years before success is a part of your name. It may take the possibility of losing everything to gain everything. Choose to be successful by struggle instead of greed for popularity. I am reminded of scripture from the words of Moses, "Choosing rather suffer the afflictions with the people of God, than to enjoy the pleasures of sin for a season." (Hebrews 11:25).

Your mission should be clear and straightforward. As we look at Moses, his directions were clear from God. In other words, he had to do what The Lord told him to do. Although you may not understand your assignment, focus on building a true relationship through obedience to God. This is a vital tool to leadership and godly success. Obedience is the call! The call is not for you to just say you're called, but to walk in the vocation of your calling. Godly obedience opens the door to so many other opportunities, and many will see your acts through love.

So, work while it's day. Work while grace is upon you. Learn what you need to learn. Then, continue to learn.

Love is Key

Condemnation seems always to bring people to a place of miss-understanding. Questions like, "Why me... Why this... Why now?" These questions all are constantly ringing in the ears of many. Truthfully, there is so much information to be gleaned from answers to these questions. Have you ever been at a place in your life when you just wanted to know why God would even choose you to become a leader? I know that I had many reasons as to why I was not qualified to lead even a bee to a flower garden. There were so many blemishes on my spiritual resume that I thought would disqualify me. My upbringing, my experiences, my downfalls, errors and my mistakes were all seen on my spiritual resume. Nevertheless, when I am reminded of The Scriptures, I had to remind myself again that while man looks on the outward appearance, God looks at the heart. All of those blemishes are removed by The Blood of Jesus.

The truth of the matter is this: It is much easier to hide behind a lie than to deal with the truth of life! Just as the case with Moses. It could have been easy for him just to say no! Remember, Moses was a murderer!! Wow! One would think that would be his ticket to tell The Lord, "I'm disqualified because of my past." Nevertheless, his condition was not the conclusion. This is true for you as well. Despite the failures and issues, God's love surpasses it all. He chose you to lead. If you accept it, you accept His love and grace.

Only The Lord knows the plans that He has for every one of us. He plans to see us be prosperous, full of wisdom, wealth and health. The design of The Lord is not for us to only exist. It's for us to be fruitful in all our areas; to be an asset and not a liability to anyone. God, The Father, always intended for us to be self-sufficient and motivators. He never intended for us just to be lumps of log.

The purpose of your calling is to prove to the world that The Lord can take the worst and make the best of you! The purpose of your calling is to share and demonstrate the love of Christ to others. Stop allowing your past to dictate your future. If your sins were blood washed, then there is no reason to allow it to haunt your present existence. If The Lord has already forgotten your sins, there should be no reminder given by anyone or anything. The most important fact is that you cannot make God remember what He has already forgotten. This fact is not true with most so-called believers in Jesus Christ. Most so-called Christians always see the sin committed and forgot the love and grace of God available. As leaders learning from leaders, we must see the sin, but forget the sin when your brother or sister confesses their sin to The Lord. The Lord casts our sins as far as the east is from the west (Psalm 103:12). We must forgive as well and demonstrate the love of God even with leaders.

Record Everything

As a mentee, you should be like a camcorder. As your leader teaches and trains you, duplicate the good things. Don't duplicate the bad things. The simplest things you learn from your leader can be something that lasts a lifetime. A pastor said, "Every good man always carries a pen." I gave this quote to my firstborn son, Ron Jr., during his early years of life. Now as an adult, I asked him one day if he remembers me telling him anything worth remembering. He responded, "Every good man always carries a pen." And you know what; he always carries a pen as well. Ron Jr. could have easily said something bogus like, "Dad your nuts," but he hinged on the very words that came out of my mouth.

As a leader, you must record everything including small statements as mentioned in the previous example. Why is this important? It's important because someone is recording you as well. Someone is tracking what you say and do. While you're duplicating someone, someone will eventually duplicate you. We are to imitate Christ; imitate our leaders. We should be eager in great expectation of hearing what The Word of God has to say to us through them for someone is eager to hear from us too.

If we would just adhere to what the messenger is trying to convey through The Scripture, we would surely benefit from the constructive criticism. One should never be afraid to face challenges in areas they are not familiar with. None of us know the capabilities we have except we go through the growing pains of life. Each day we should try to familiarize ourselves with many new and exciting tactics that we would normally ignore. Many of our challenges are not as challenging as we deem them to be. Often, the solutions are right in front of us.

God Uses People

God is looking for people that can relate to this truth: God is the source, and we are the resource for someone else to be blessed. He uses people to minister to others.

To be used of The Lord, take the time to look in the mirror and ask yourself the question, "Did I put in enough time with The Source to become His resource?" Answering this question too quickly can result in disaster. I say this because I don't believe there has ever been one real God-called leader who will say, "I was eager to do what God mandated for me to do." Why? Because when we count the cost of doing ministry and the cross we have to bear, I don't think any leader can be eager. It is my opinion that there were many times in the forty years that Moses was in preparation for the eighty years of him leading the people of God that he felt inadequate. I believe this to be a normal feeling of every leader. I know it was for me. I was told that success is failure upside down. You have to have faith and allow God to use you so that failures can be turned into success.

I never had the full aspirations of being a leader. I - more or less - wanted to be a leader without having the full responsibility of a leader. I liked the idea that I was no longer a follower and had graduated to the stage where I could lead someone else. At the same time, the whole idea of me being a leader was funny to me. The way leadership came about in my life was even funny. I was not the brightest in the bunch, nor did I confess to being the brightest in the bunch. I graduated from High School by the very skin of my teeth. I was most likely not to succeed in life and bound to be a blue collar worker. My downfalls and failures as a teenager and young adult became my stepping stone to a bright future in my adulthood. This could only happen through The Source.

There should be much encouragement through my testimony for you. Like me, God will rain on those who may not be the brightest. If you have a willing heart to be trained, corrected and loved, God will work through you. He did it for me. I often sit in my office at the church and ponder about how I got to this place. I may not pastor the largest congregation, but the people follow me as I follow Christ.

One of the Mother's in Zion and one of my first members, the Late Mildred Bieard, she left a church she was serving for over 30 years to join my church. One day, in my curiosity I asked her, "Mother, why did you choose to follow my ministry?" She replied, "The Word of God and the preaching of The Gospel of Jesus Christ is pure and true." I don't state this to brag, but I state it to bring out a point. If you as a leader stick to the plan God has set, He will direct people to follow to authenticate you and the call upon your life. Like Moses, The Israelites followed Moses. He too wasn't perfect as we know. Yet, the people followed. Even when they sinned or caused problems, they returned to Moses and his leadership because he was connected to The Source.

You are Chosen

Receiving the call of God is much different than answering the call of God. Let's say your cellphone starts chiming. You are receiving a call. However, you must decide if you're going to answer the call. There are many people who know they are called by God, but won't respond or answer the call. The dream and confirmation I received from my pastor regarding my call to the ministry was the call for me, but I had to answer. I had to realize that I was chosen.

We know that many are called but few are chosen (Matthew 22:14). My initial goal in the church was just to be a deacon in the church. I wanted to take my place in the church; sit on the front row at church, and assist the pastor with the needs of the church. Yet, I was chosen. While the deacon staff has a very important responsibility in the church, The Lord needed me elsewhere. I had to pick up the phone and receive instructions from The Lord for my life. I had to accept that I was chosen.

Moses did not stop at the burning bush. He moved from there with God, stayed with God, and God worked through Him. He became the resource for The Israelites to be delivered from Egypt. He also became a resource of learning for us today.

As a leader of today, the trials and tribulations that faced Moses are similar to many I had to face in leadership. I've never felt as though I was a leader. I've always felt like I should keep quiet and let others do. Through my eyes, I felt inadequate, immature, and childish, but through God, I became more than what others thought of me and what statistics said I would be. I became and will continue to be: One of God's Chosen Leaders.

As you tackle leadership, don't do it alone. Let God's presence lead you. Don't let your imagination and worries turn you away from your destiny. It's time for you to pick up the phone. You hear The Lord calling. Pick up your phone and respond to His calling. You are chosen. You may count yourself worthless through your eyes, but in God's eyes – you are the apple of His eye.

About the Author

Dr. Ronald S. Hobson, Sr., Ph.D.

A native of North Bellport, New York, and a Veteran of the United States Army, Dr. Ronald S. Hobson, Sr., Ph.D. is an ordained licensed minister of The Gospel for over 29 years. He attended Empire State College with a concentration in Business Administration and attended the University of Phoenix with a concentration in Psychology. Later, he received an honorary Doctorate of Divinity from Abundant Life Bible College & Theological Seminary.

He was reared in The Church of God in Christ under the leadership and spiritual guidance of Bishop Ralph L. Jefferson, D.D. (Jefferson Temple C.O.G.I.C., North Bellport, New York).

Dr. Hobson has served in many capacities upon accepting His call to the ministry. He has served as Senior Pastor & Founder of Mission of Deliverance Worship Center (Later named Refreshing Spring Worship Center, Baltimore, Maryland in 2006) for over 15 years.

He currently serves as Senior Pastor of The Fellowship Church, Charlotte, North Carolina. He is also serving as the National Chairman of Men's Ministry for United Fellowship of Christian Churches & Ministries, Inc. He is a Member of the Sacred College of Bishops (United

Fellowship of Christian Churches and Ministries - UFCCM); he is a former member of Gateway Pastors Association, Dundalk, Maryland; a former member of Dundalk Pastors Association; and a member of American Foreign Legion, Dundalk, Maryland; and a current member of Veterans of Foreign Wars, Baltimore, Maryland. He also a graduate and serves as the Vice-President of Encouraging Faith Theological University, Ocala, Florida.

While Dr. Hobson has served many people in many areas, his one true vision remains the same: To promote The Kingdom of God through training, teaching and spreading The Gospel of Jesus Christ to everyone around the world.

Connecting with the Author

Dr. Ronald S. Hobson, Sr., Ph.D.

Mailing Address: 2208 Hanfred Lane, Suite 101-17, Tucker, GA 30084

Ministry Number: (470) 673-5877

Fax Number: (770) 881-7654

Ministry Email: SctHobs@gmail.com

Ministry Website: www.powernetwork.tv/tfc

Online School: www.eftuonline.com

Social Media

Facebook: Ronald S Hobson
Twitter: Rhobsonsr
Periscope: @RHobsonsr